Improving Your Prayer Life

by

Roger Pugh

To Megan and David

*"...the effectual fervent prayer
of a righteous man availeth much."
James 5:16b KJV*

Table of Contents

Preface

How do you improve your prayer life? This book offers suggestions that are based on Scripture and strategies gleaned from praying friends and my personal experience with prayer. Each chapter begins with Scripture and includes explanation and application. The primary goal of this book is to provide a resource that people can use to improve their prayer lives over time. Each time you read it you can learn new things, be reminded of points you already know, and be refreshed and motivated to pray. My prayer is that this book will bless you, enrich your prayer life and help you draw nearer to God.

Roger Pugh
January 2019

Part One: Improving Your Prayer Life by Believing in the Potential of Your Prayer Life

Praying in Faith

Then the disciples came to Jesus privately and said, "Why could we not cast it out?" He said to them, "Because of your little faith. For truly, I say to you, if you have faith like a grain of mustard seed, you will say to this mountain, 'Move from here to there,' and it will move, and nothing will be impossible for you." Matthew 17:19-20

Therefore I tell you, whatever you ask in prayer, believe that you have received it, and it will be yours. Mark 11:24

The disciples had a problem. They could not cast out a demon. Jesus easily cast it out and then instructed them on the importance of faith. Faith is especially important in the area of prayer. When we pray to God in faith, nothing will be impossible for us.

According to Hebrews 11:1, faith is the substance of things hoped for and the conviction of things not seen. Praying faith is an inner conviction that God will work as we pray. The result will be receiving the substance of what we prayed to receive. We can have this conviction as God communicates what He desires to do either through His Word or through the leading of the Holy Spirit. Praying what God desires to do will always assure the answer! The conviction is because God told us what He desires, and the substance comes because God always says yes to what He Himself has prompted us to pray.[1] Sometimes praying in faith enables us to move a mountain immediately. But keep trusting God even if the answer does not come right away.[2] Praying what God desires guarantees His answer.

While God always delights to answer our prayers, some things are not His purpose for us. So when we do not know His heart on a matter, we may or may not get what we are asking Him to give. This is different from praying in faith in what God has shown us He wants to do.[3] If we are praying without specific direction from God, He may answer yes,[4] no,[5] or, wait.[6]

Utilize the power of praying God's will. Ask God to show you what to ask. Listen to God as you study the Bible, and listen to the Holy Spirit. Pray and anticipate His answer.

---

[1] For further information on this Scripture, see Roger Pugh, *Hearing God's Voice and Responding in Faith: a Commentary on Hebrews* (Colombia, South Carolina: Createspace, 2017).
[2] Luke 18:1-8 - I knew one man who came to Christ for salvation in his 80's. His family had prayed for him for decades.
[3] God communicates what He desires through Scripture and through the Holy Spirit's leading - Psalm 119:105, Acts 10:19-20, Acts 8:29.
[4] Mark 1:40-42; Exodus 33:18-23 (a yes answer with conditions)
[5] 2 Corinthians 12:8-9
[6] Acts 1:6-8; Numbers 12:13-14

Satisfying Our Longings

Then they cried to the LORD in their trouble, and he delivered them from their distress. He led them by a straight way till they reached a city to dwell in. Let them thank the LORD for his steadfast love, for his wondrous works to the children of man! For he satisfies the longing soul, and the hungry soul he fills with good things. Psalm 107:6-9

Trust that God can satisfy your longings through your prayer time with Him. The most profound need of the human heart is a relationship with God. Often we look to other things or to people to satisfy us, but God is the only person who truly can satisfy our souls. In prayer, we relate to God. As we pray in the Spirit, we are drawn into close fellowship with God and edified in His presence. He satisfies us like nothing else and no one else.

God delights to satisfy specific longings or desires in our lives because he loves us. Sometimes He does this directly by giving us an answer to prayer. But other times, God satisfies our longings by saying no to the prayer we have asked so that He can give us what He knows is better. God created us, so He knows perfectly how we tick and what is best for us. One of the remarkable things I have discovered is that God has redirected me from what I initially thought I wanted to enjoy to what He knew I truly wanted instead. Because He loves us, we can trust Him to lead us in the right way and to satisfy our longings at the right time that He knows is best. The greatest fulfillment of this will be in eternity as we experience the place that Christ has prepared for us.

Draw near to God because you want to be close to Him. Close fellowship with Him satisfies as nothing else can. Ask God for the specific things you long for in your life. Trust that He will give them to you or that He will say no and give you something better. Ultimately, trust that your greatest delights and fulfillment will come when Jesus comes to take us to our new home in heaven.[7]

---

[7] 1 Corinthians 2:9

Bringing Deliverance in Trouble

Then they cried to the LORD in their trouble, and he delivered them from their distress. Psalm 107:13
I sought the LORD, and he answered me and delivered me from all my fears. Psalm 34:4

When you are experiencing trouble in your life, take your concerns to God in prayer. He specializes in delivering us from our problems and sustaining us through them.

First, cry out to Him. Tell Him your problem and the specifics of what you are facing. Pour out your heart to Him and vent to Him. He is never shocked by what we feel because He already knows it. Instead, He is delighted that we have come to spend time with Him.

Second, include prayers of thanks with your requests.[8] God uses your thanks to change your attitudes and redirect your focus to Him and His goodness. As you thank and praise God, His power is released to help you spiritually and to overcome the challenges you face.[9]

Third, seek the Lord relationally. The encouragement and grace that you receive by drawing near to Him can give you the strength you need to face your trouble. Ask Him to fill you with the Holy Spirit, and ask the Holy Spirit to connect with God through you. Sometimes we are distracted and struggle to focus on God because we are focused

---

[8] Philippians 4:6-7
[9] 2 Chronicles 20:20-22

on problems. The Spirit helps us overcome distraction so that we can be encouraged by fellowship with God. But as He helps us with fellowship, He also guides us[10] and prays for us[11] so that we can make good decisions. Seek the Lord relationally toward the beginning of your time with God, and you will find that the rest of your time with God is more meaningful. As you draw near to Him, He draws near to you.[12] As He draws near to you, His supernatural power is released to deliver you or sustain you in trouble.[13]

---

[10] Colossians 3:15
[11] Romans 8:26-27
[12] James 4:8
[13] 1 Samuel 17:47

Finding Freedom

Some sat in darkness and in the shadow of death, prisoners in affliction and in irons, for they had rebelled against the words of God, and spurned the counsel of the Most High. So he bowed their hearts down with hard labor; they fell down, with none to help. Then they cried to the LORD in their trouble, and he delivered them from their distress. He brought them out of darkness and the shadow of death, and burst their bonds apart. Let them thank the LORD for his steadfast love, for his wondrous works to the children of man! For he shatters the doors of bronze and cuts in two the bars of iron. Psalm 107:10-16

Is not this the fast that I choose: to loose the bonds of wickedness, to undo the straps of the yoke, to let the oppressed go free, and to break every yoke? Isaiah 58:6

Often people are bound to sin, negative emotions, or to consequences as God disciplines them. God specializes in setting us free as we bring these things to Him in prayer.[14]

First, tell Him about the bondage in your life and ask Him to set you free. Since God cares deeply for us, He delights to help us. Be specific about your struggles, attitudes, and situations as you pray.

---

[14] This chapter addresses people who have a relationship with Jesus Christ. If you have not yet begun a relationship with Him, see the chapter on page 37 entitled, "Receiving a Relationship."

Telling God specifically about things enables you to see when He answers and helps you not to miss His help in any area.[15] Confess and repent of any sin. Confession is simply telling God, "I sinned when I _____." It is admitting your sin to Him.[16] Repentance is a genuine choice to turn from sin and obey God. You may need to ask Him to change your heart so that you can genuinely repent.

In particularly difficult cases, fasting and prayer can help break strongholds.[17] Fasting helps us connect with God more closely and to hear Him more clearly. It also is named as a tool God uses to break strongholds.[18] Check with your doctor to make sure you are healthy enough to fast before doing so. Also, be sure to drink plenty of fluids. If you are fasting for several days, you may want to drink juice for some energy a few times a day.

Second, enlist a trusted and godly person of the same sex to pray for you.[19] God uses your confession to bring your sin into the light and to help the person understand your need. Confess sin generally[20] rather than explicitly, trusting God to answer appropriately. Too much detail can tempt or overwhelm the other person. All he or she needs is enough information to know what struggle to ask God to heal. God will use the prayer of a friend to set you free.

---

[15] James 4:2
[16] 1 John 1:9
[17] Isaiah 58:6, 2 Corinthians 10:3-5
[18] See the Scripture above.
[19] James 5:16
[20] Galatians 6:1

14

Third, seek God's counsel in the Bible. Search God's Word to learn how to deal with your problem. Jesus said, "You will know the truth and the truth will set you free."[21] Ask God to give you the wisdom to overcome what you are facing.[22]

Pray fervently and persistently for deliverance, and keep your sins confessed, even the sins of attitude.[23] Trust that God will set you free.[24]

Fourth, rely on the Holy Spirit to help you. Ask Him to strengthen you when you are tempted or bound in sin. Ask Him to help you fully surrender to Him and trust Him. Request that He lead you in what to do when you are struggling. Follow His leading in steps to take, precautions to follow, and the right activity to substitute for the path you are tempted to take.[25]

---

[21] John 8:32
[22] James 1:5
[23] For a helpful book on different sin categories, see Gregory Frizzell and K. N. Rowland, *Returning to Holiness: a Personal and Churchwide Journey to Revival* (Master Design, 2001).
[24] John 8:36
[25] Galatians 5:16

Experiencing Healing

Some were fools through their sinful ways, and because of their iniquities suffered affliction; they loathed any kind of food, and they drew near to the gates of death. Then they cried to the LORD in their trouble, and he delivered them from their distress. He sent out his word and healed them, and delivered them from their destruction. Psalm 107:17-20

...I am the LORD, your healer. Exodus 15:26

When you are sick, remember that God heals through prayer. Even when the illness is due to sin, God often still heals according to His wisdom and love. He can say yes, no, or wait to our prayers for healing. But He will definitely heal all believers when Jesus comes to take them to heaven.[26] When healing is delayed, He gives us the grace we need to deal with the problem while we wait.[27]

I have witnessed God's healing power as well as his grace in sustaining church members through illness.

Several years ago, a church member fell and hit her head during a church cantata. This resulted in brain swelling which required insertion of a permanent feeding tube. When it came time to remove the tube, her husband asked why surgery was required. Doctors told him the type of feeding

---

[26] 1 Thessalonians 4:13-18
[27] 2 Corinthians 12:7-10

tube used on his wife is used when they do not expect a recovery. She is still doing well.

Another man we prayed for in our church was told he would never recover from debilitating headaches and that he would never again be able to work. He recently went for a job interview because he is cured and able to work.[28]

Years ago, a church I attended celebrated the healing of a woman who had a softball-sized cancer in her abdomen. The doctors had found it as they scanned and ran tests. Yet on the day they were going to do surgery, it was completely gone! Many churches had been praying, and God answered.

God can even bless us by saying no to our prayer for healing. A woman in a former church had to have both legs amputated. She shared with me that through her illness, God restored her relationship with her sister. Her heart was filled with gratitude to God for her amputations because of the mended relationship.

Take your sickness to Jesus in prayer. He delights to heal us and help us in sickness. Trust in God's healing power, and trust Him to work on your behalf even when he says no or wait.

---

[28] Both of these stories were told in public worship services to give glory to God for what He has done.

Embracing Spiritual Healing

Is anyone among you sick? Let him call for the elders of the church, and let them pray over him, anointing him with oil in the name of the Lord. And the prayer of faith will save the one who is sick, and the Lord will raise him up. And if he has committed sins, he will be forgiven. Therefore, confess your sins to one another and pray for one another, that you may be healed. The prayer of a righteous person has great power as it is working. Elijah was a man with a nature like ours, and he prayed fervently that it might not rain, and for three years and six months, it did not rain on the earth. Then he prayed again, and heaven gave rain, and the earth bore its fruit. My brothers, if anyone among you wanders from the truth and someone brings him back, let him know that whoever brings back a sinner from his wandering will save his soul from death and will cover a multitude of sins. James 5:14-20

Sometimes physical sickness is a symptom of spiritual sickness. If you think this might be the case in your life, confess your sins to people you trust and ask them to pray for your spiritual and physical healing.

The prayer of a righteous[29] person is very powerful to affect spiritual change. Elijah is an example of this. Through his prayers for the rain to

---

[29] "Righteous person" means a person who generally does what is right.

stop,[30] God brought judgment that humbled the nation and ultimately brought repentance at Mount Carmel. Then Elijah prayed again, and God restored the rain.[31]

Our prayers can bring a wandering sinner back, save his soul from death, and cover a multitude of sins through his repentance. Do you know people who are wandering from God? Pray for them. Supernatural change can come to the people you love through your prayers.

When you begin to wander or struggle with sin, tell God and ask Him to bring genuine repentance and surrender to your heart.[32] Ask Him to help you hunger and thirst after righteousness[33] and seek Him with all your heart.[34]

When your sins begin to overwhelm you, cry out to God for help.[35] Also, recognize the amazing resource that God has given to you through your trustworthy[36] brothers and sisters in Christ who also can pray for you. Spiritual healing is available for those who will bring their concern to God in prayer.

---

[30] 1 Kings 17:1
[31] 1 Kings 18
[32] Psalm 51:10
[33] Matthew 5:6
[34] Jeremiah 29:13
[35] Psalm 40:11-13
[36] When you confess your sin, do so with people who are not gossips. See Proverbs 11:13.

Enjoying Emotional Healing

*The LORD builds up Jerusalem; he gathers the
outcasts of Israel. He heals the brokenhearted and
binds up their wounds. Psalms 147:2-3*

*The LORD is near to the brokenhearted and
saves the crushed in spirit. Psalms 34:18*

God heals us emotionally, and He is uniquely
equipped to do so because He created our emotions.
We can ask for healing and use the spiritual tools
God has given to us to overcome emotional
brokenness. Depending on the severity of our
brokenness, the process may take some time, but He
is able to heal us.

Ask God to build you up emotionally since this is
what He delights to do. God builds us up
emotionally through His Word, through fellowship
with other believers, and through specific acts of
encouragement that He brings to us to help us when
we are struggling. As you ask God to heal you,
choose to be in His Word, with God's people, and
anticipate God's answers to your prayers for
encouragement.

Tell God about your problems and challenges,
and ask Him to intervene. Mix thanksgiving
together with your requests until God brings His
peace.[37] Many times in the Psalms, David goes to
God with his burdens, grief, and pain; and God lifts
him up and builds him up in His presence. The
entire mood of the Psalm shifts from one of

---

37 Philippians 4:6-7

complaint to one of worship.[38] Praying the Psalms to God is one way you can tell God about your struggles.

Praising and thanking God are great ways to be built up emotionally. Since God inhabits the praises of His people,[39] His presence will minister to you as you praise[40] and thank[41] Him.

Sometimes emotional healing can come when we understand God's heart toward us. Psalm 139 explains God's personal concern for His people, His creation of them in the womb, and His record of all their days before any of them came to be. Try praying Scriptures like Psalm 139 to God and find comfort in His heart for you. You will also be thanking and praising God for what He has done as you pray it to Him.

Ask God to heal you when you are brokenhearted and wounded emotionally. Tell Him about your pain, and ask Him for what you need. If you don't know what you need, ask Him to give you what He knows is best. Since He is our good shepherd, He knows exactly how to minister to His sheep.[42]

Above all, remember that He is near to you when you are broken. Regardless of how you may feel,

---

[38] See Psalm 77 as an example.

[39] Psalm 22:3 KJV

[40] Praise is simply telling God something you appreciate about who He is. For example, you could say, "I praise you Lord for your great faithfulness and kindness to me. You are always here for me when I pray to you."

[41] Thanks can be for spiritual, physical, relational, vocational, or future blessings.

[42] John 10:11-14, Psalm 23

God has not abandoned you. Trust Him to help you and deliver you as you seek Him.[43]

---

[43] Psalm 34:18

Part Two: Improving Your Prayer Life by Understanding What Prayer Is

Defining Prayer

To Seth also a son was born, and he called his name Enosh. At that time people began to call upon the name of the LORD. Genesis 4:26

Prayer is simply talking to God and listening to Him. Since God is a person, He wants to interact with us as His people. We are told to cast our cares on Him because He cares for us.[44] Tell Him about your worries, your painful situations, your struggles, and your broken relationships because He cares.

Understand that God intends prayer to be a friendship with Him.[45] Abraham was called the friend of God because he had a close relationship with God.[46] Many times, God shared with Abraham what He was going to do[47] or what He wanted Abraham to do.[48] Abraham asked God for things,[49] told God about the situations he didn't understand,[50] and praised God for the good things that God had done for Him.[51]

When we pray, we enter God's presence in His heavenly dwelling place.[52] Wherever we may be physically; when we pray we are personally relating

---

[44] 1 Peter 5:7
[45] John 15:15
[46] James 2:23
[47] Genesis 12, 15, 17, 22
[48] Genesis 12:1
[49] Genesis 18:23-33
[50] Genesis 15:2
[51] Genesis 22:14
[52] Hebrews 6:19; Ephesians 2:4-6

to Him. We have an audience with God spirit to spirit. This is possible because Jesus has prepared the way for us at the cross.[53] He ripped the veil at the Temple in Jerusalem so that we would know that the way is open to come into the very presence of God in the heavenly temple.[54] If you have chosen to turn from sin and receive the gift of eternal life, the way is always open for you to come into the presence of God. Thank and praise God for the incredible opening He has made into His presence through Jesus' work.

Prayer also is warfare.[55] Through talking to God and praying for others, we fight a spiritual fight to overcome Satan's desires to destroy us, our families, our churches, and our nations. If someone is tempted, pray for her. If someone is discouraged, pray for him. As God brings people to mind, pray for them. God told Ezekiel that He was looking for someone to pray for the city but could find no one. So He destroyed it.[56]

When you think about prayer, remember you are talking to God, listening to God, building a friendship, entering His presence in heaven, and fighting a war against the Enemy of your soul, the Devil.

---

[53] Matthew 27:46-51; John 19:30; Hebrews 6:19-20
[54] Matthew 27:46-51; Hebrews 9:24; Ephesians 2:4-6
[55] Ephesians 6:18
[56] Ezekiel 22:30-31

Learning to Listen

And let the peace of Christ rule in your hearts, to which indeed you were called in one body. And be thankful. Let the word of Christ dwell in you richly, teaching and admonishing one another in all wisdom, singing psalms and hymns and spiritual songs, with thankfulness in your hearts to God. Colossians 3:15-16

Let your reasonableness be known to everyone. The Lord is at hand; do not be anxious about anything, but in everything by prayer and supplication with thanksgiving let your requests be made known to God. And the peace of God, which surpasses all understanding, will guard your hearts and your minds in Christ Jesus. Philippians 4:5-7

For God is not a God of confusion but of peace. 1 Corinthians 14:33

We can significantly improve our prayer lives by learning to listen to God. We listen to God in two primary ways. Hear as He speaks through the Scriptures and through the leading of the Holy Spirit. Some groups within the church deny the leading of the Spirit and others deny the Scriptures in preference to leading of the Spirit. But really, the two are inseparable. The Scripture is the sword the Spirit uses in our lives.[57] And since the Scripture is what the Spirit has clearly said,[58] Scripture takes

---

[57] Ephesians 6:17-18
[58] 2 Peter 1:19-21; 2 Timothy 3:16-17

precedence over every other communication from God.[59]

We need to listen to the Scripture as we hear it or read it. Seek to understand what the Scripture intends to communicate in the original context in which it was written. Ask God to show you what is timeless[60] to apply to your life and then obey it.

Sometimes the Spirit will apply Scripture in a particular way to your life. As you are reading, you come across a verse that leaps off the page. Perhaps it is something you just asked God about in your prayer time. Maybe you have been struggling, and it addresses your struggle explicitly. It could be that God takes a Scripture and applies it to you through the touch of the Spirit upon your heart to encourage you or lift you up in some way. In these cases, the Word of God becomes the means of a special communication of the Spirit to your heart.

As God desires, the Spirit will lead you in making a decision through bringing a sense of peace to your heart concerning the right course of action.[61] Use caution with this. Pray for at least several days concerning an important decision. If you flip-flop on your decision, it is not peace from the Spirit; it is your changing emotion.[62] The Holy Spirit does not

---

[59] Isaiah 8:20

[60] Isaiah 40:8

[61] See Colossians 3:15-16 above.

[62] Leadership from the Spirit should never be used as an excuse to cause fighting in the church. If the Spirit is leading you, He is able to change the minds of others. You do not need to try to do His job for Him. With these things in mind, let the peace of God rule in your heart. See Philippians 4:5-7.

confuse us but is consistently clear as we seek Him.[63]

God also may at times speak to you through another person or group of people such as your local church body.[64] Again, use caution in this. If God can speak to you through another person, He can also confirm it to you in your heart. See 1 Kings 13 for an example of the danger of listening to someone else when God has something different in mind. However, many times in Scripture God uses someone to share a message. If you recognize this, you can significantly benefit from the encouragement of God's people. God has spoken in my life through conversations with other Christians, through messages shared at church, through books, and through songs. The Biblical book of Proverbs was written with the assumption that we can hear from God through others.[65] The description of the prophetic office in Scripture also confirms this. In the New Testament, we have speaking gifts listed such as encouragement, teaching, prophecy,[66] and pastor-teacher. If God has given speaking gifts, it follows that He means for us to listen to others in the assembly with the recognition that God may speak through them. The Holy Spirit will confirm what is said to your heart with His touch upon your spirit or through Scripture as you seek Him.

---

[63] See 1 Corinthians 14:33 above.
[64] See Colossians 3:15-16 above.
[65] Proverbs 1:1-9
[66] Prophecy in the New Testament is the sharing of what God has laid upon your heart to encourage others or build them up in some way. See 1 Corinthians 14.

Thank God for loving you enough to communicate with you and encourage you through His Scripture, His peace, and His assembly of believers He has given for your edification![67] Believe the promises God has given to those who listen to Him.[68]

---

[67] Other examples are given in Scripture such as God sending an angel, but the examples I have given are the more primary ways God speaks. Again, all of these communications must be in agreement with Scripture.

[68] Psalm 81:10-16 shows us that God brings blessing to our lives when we listen to Him. The book of Hebrews also emphasizes that it is through listening to God and responding in faith that we enter God's rest - Hebrews 4:1-3. See also Psalm 25:12.

Knowing How to Pray

...Lord, teach us to pray, as John taught his disciples. Luke 11:1

After hearing this request from His disciples, Jesus gave them what has been called, "The Lord's Prayer." Each segment teaches something on how we should pray. We are to follow Jesus' example.

Jesus prayed, "Father, hallowed be your name."[69] We are to show our love for God by addressing Him as the good and perfect Father that He is. We are also to desire that His name is honored and set apart as holy in our lives and in the lives of others. This is an attitude of praise and worship of the greatness of our God, but also shows our love for God because we care what others think of Him.

Next, Jesus prayed, "Your kingdom come."[70] We are to pray for the things of God's kingdom to increase and thrive in this world. This includes praying for lost people to be saved, praying for our churches, and praying for the growth of God's people. It also includes praying for missionaries and sister churches. But we are also to long for the coming of the consummated[71] kingdom of Christ in the future.[72]

---

[69] Luke 11:2
[70] Ibid.
[71] Jesus' will reign in the eternal state with a new heaven, new earth, and new Jerusalem.
[72] Revelation 11:15, 19:11-21, 21:1-4

Then Jesus prayed, "Give us each day our daily bread."[73] We are to ask God for the things that we need physically, spiritually, and emotionally. God wants to supply all our needs,[74] but may not grant all our wants if He knows they are not in our best interest or the interests of His kingdom.[75] Ask God for what you need.

Also, Jesus prayed, "...and forgive us our sins, for we ourselves forgive everyone who is indebted to us."[76] We need to pray for forgiveness and have a forgiving heart toward others. This is critical to a healthy prayer life. Our closeness to God relationally depends on our forgiveness of others. An unforgiving heart is a sin against God. Tell God that you are no longer holding that other person responsible for the wrong done to you. You are canceling whatever is owed. Make the relationship right if you can. But even if a restored relationship is not possible, forgive the person. Be wise in your relationships with those who have wronged you, and take steps to protect yourself if the person has not repented. But let it go. Otherwise, it will hinder your relationship with God and your prayer life. Then confess your sins to God.[77]

Additionally, Jesus prayed, "...and lead us not into temptation."[78] We are to pray for deliverance from temptation. This is part of the warfare

---

73 Luke 11:3
74 Matthew 6:32; Philippians 4:19
75 2 Corinthians 12:8-9
76 Luke 11:4
77 1 John 1:9
78 Luke 11:4

mentioned previously. We pray for protection from the influence of the world, our old nature, and the Devil. God can reduce our temptation if we ask Him to do so.[79]

Also, note that this prayer is prayed collectively with the word, "us." Pray these things for others within your local church assembly and around the world.

---

[79] Some temptation will come in this life - see 1 Corinthians 10:13.

Part Three: Improving Your Prayer Life by Dealing with Barriers to Healthy Prayer

Receiving a Relationship

But to all who did receive him, who believed in his name, he gave the right to become children of God. John 1:12

Having a relationship with God is the first and most crucial step to improving your prayer life. God hears prayers that people who do not know Him pray and sometimes He graciously answers. However, power and intimacy in prayer are for those who know Him.

Receiving a relationship with God begins with knowing a few things that God says. God says that all of us have sinned.[80] Sin is anything we say, do, or don't do that is displeasing to God.[81] We also need to understand that our sin makes us guilty before God and separates us from God so that a relationship with Him is impossible apart from what Jesus Christ has done for us.

The Bible says, "But God shows his love for us in that while we were still sinners, Christ died for us" Romans 5:8. God loves us despite our sin, and He has made a way for us to have a relationship with Him through Jesus' death at the cross. Jesus died to pay for our sin. He took our punishment on Himself so that we could have a relationship with God.

The Bible also says, "For the wages of sin is death, but the free gift of God is eternal life in Christ Jesus

---

[80] Romans 3:23
[81] I got this phrase from the Everyday Evangelism Training in an Evangelism Explosion course.

our Lord" Romans 6:23. Our sin earns us death spiritually and eternally. Spiritual death is our separation from God relationally. And eternal death is the eternal punishment for sins in the lake of fire that Revelation 20:14 describes. Jesus' death at the cross included separation from God relationally[82] and the wrath[83] and justice[84] of God for our sin that was placed on Him. Jesus paid it all[85] even though He lived a perfect life without sin. Then He rose from the dead. We can receive eternal life as a gift because of what Jesus has done.

Receiving eternal life includes two steps. First, we must decide to surrender our lives to Christ. The Bible calls this repentance.[86] This is a choice that we make to follow Jesus instead of the path of sin or our own way. Second, we need to put our trust in God's promise that He will give us eternal life through Jesus' death for our sin. Eternal life is the new life God gives us spiritually the moment we enter into a relationship with Him,[87] but it is also the hope of being resurrected to enjoy a new life with Him in a New Heaven, New Earth, and New Jerusalem.[88]

If you would like to receive a relationship with God, ask God to help you genuinely surrender to Him and put your trust in what Jesus has done to

---

[82] Matthew 27:46
[83] 1 John 4:10
[84] 1 Peter 3:18
[85] John 19:30
[86] Luke 13:3; Romans 10:9-10
[87] John 17:3
[88] Revelation 21:1-2

pay for your sin. If this prayer expresses the desire of your heart, pray: *Jesus, I have done wrong, and I need your forgiveness. I choose to turn from my sin and to surrender my life to follow you. I believe that you will forgive me and give me eternal life because of what you did for me at the cross. I believe you rose from the dead. I trust you to keep your promise, and I receive you, Jesus, as the only one who can save me from judgment and give me the gift of eternal life. Come into my life and make me what you want me to be. Thank you for giving me the gift of eternal life.*

If you prayed this prayer, find a Bible-believing church in your area, read the Bible if you have access to one, and begin daily praying to God. Other believers can help you and encourage you in your walk with God. Time reading Scripture and praying will help you grow in your walk with God.

Confessing Sin

If we confess our sins, he is faithful and just to forgive us our sins and to cleanse us from all unrighteousness. 1 John 1:9

Once you have a relationship with God, it is eternal. But sometimes your relationship can be hindered with God through sin. For example, when you fight with your family, you usually have to make things right with them to restore the closeness in your family. The same thing is true with God. If you have a sin in your life, confession is simply telling God about it. If you tell Him, He is always faithful to forgive our sin by restoring the relationship. Of course, if you harbor sin in your heart, you can still hinder your relationship with God. Tell Him exactly what you are thinking and feeling, and ask Him to change your heart. Ask Him to fill you with the Holy Spirit. To be filled with the Holy Spirit is to be controlled and led by Him. Then ask the Holy Spirit to surrender through you and trust God through you.[89] He will help you by empowering you to live for God.

Some categories of sin you might need to confess include anything you have done that you know is wrong; anything that you wrongly have failed to do; anything that you have said that dishonors God or tears down people; and, any bad attitude or

---

[89] For these steps on how to be filled with the Holy Spirit, see further: Jack Graham, *Powering Up* (Wheaton: Crossway Publishers, 2009), 77-92.

bitterness that you hold against someone else. Listen to your conscience and the Holy Spirit's conviction within you. But once you have confessed and repented of sin, forget it because God has.

Try to keep sins confessed as they happen. If you do this, you will likely have some prayer times where confession is not necessary. If you do have unconfessed sin that you know about, it will hinder your prayer life. Confess it.[90] Now you are ready to pray without a barrier between you and God.

---

[90] If you are worried about sins you do not know about, ask God if there are any, and confess any He brings to mind. If God reveals no further sin, pray with confidence.

Overcoming Sin Habits

For though we walk in the flesh, we are not waging war according to the flesh. For the weapons of our warfare are not of the flesh but have divine power to destroy strongholds. We destroy arguments and every lofty opinion raised against the knowledge of God, and take every thought captive to obey Christ.... 2 Cor. 10:3-5

Therefore, confess your sins to one another and pray for one another, that you may be healed. The prayer of a righteous person has great power as it is working. James 5:16

Sometimes you have a sin habit that you cannot seem to conquer. Sin habits war against our souls,[91] robbing us of the abundant life that Jesus desires for us and hindering our prayer life. Though much could be said about this, I want to focus on key things to do when you find yourself struggling with a sin habit.

First, tell[92] a mature believer you trust about your struggle.[93] This person needs to care genuinely about you so that he or she will be committed to

---

[91] 1 Peter 2:11

[92] If your sin violates the law, the person you tell may have to report it to the authorities by law. Also, most people agree to keep a confidence with the understanding that you are not going to try to hurt someone else or hurt yourself. In these situations, confession will come with consequences for you but could still be helpful for you spiritually to break the hold of your sin.

[93] James 5:16

praying for you. In most cases, it's better if this person is of the same sex. Choose this person wisely and avoid sharing with anyone who gossips or has a hard time keeping things confidential. Spare them the details, but generally describe your struggle so the person can join you in prayer for spiritual freedom from the sin. Telling someone else about your struggle brings it into the light, and begins the process of healing as that person prays for you to be healed. This is a very powerful weapon to use against sin habits.

Second, ask for God's wisdom in overcoming your struggle and follow it.[94] Trust God to give you wisdom to overcome your sin because you know it is God's will.[95]

Third, make wise decisions about your temptations. Stop going to places or even close to places where you tend to fall into sin if you are able to avoid them.[96] These could be actual places in your town, or they could be electronic places on your computer or smartphone. In some cases, guarding yourself against temptation may require extreme measures. For example, one man I know got rid of his television and all other visual sources of temptation in his home. Filters can be purchased for internet and smartphones, and a password could be given to a trusted friend or family member. Consider and pray about changing jobs if you are being tempted to sin with a coworker. Don't compromise

[94] James 1:5-6
[95] John 14:13-14
[96] Proverbs 7:1-27

even a little bit in gratifying your sin nature.[97] Take your tempting situations seriously or you will continue your sin habit. Sometimes taking seemingly drastic steps is what delivers us from sin that hinders our spiritual lives.

Fourth, spend regular time in prayer,[98] God's Word,[99] and with your local assembly of believers.[100] These activities are weapons that God has given us to overcome sin habits in our lives. Using these weapons to combat and move past sin habits will encourage spiritual growth.

Fifth, ask the Holy Spirit to empower you and live in victory through you.[101] He delights to grant His power to us to help us choose the right way, but we still must choose it. He does not force it. If we choose to walk in what He desires us to do, we will not gratify our old sinful natures.[102] As we keep following the leading of the Spirit, the flesh loses its power and we live in freedom.[103] Holy Spirit empowerment is the most important step in overcoming sin habits.

Overcoming sin habits will strengthen your prayer life because you will no longer be grieving the Holy Spirit with your sin. Greater intimacy and

---

[97] Genesis 39:10

[98] Ephesians 6:18

[99] Hebrews 4:12-13

[100] Note the, "we" above in 2 Corinthians 10:3-5.

[101] Romans 8:11-13

[102] Galatians 5:16

[103] 2 Corinthians 3:17 - This freedom is in seasons of time, but one day will be complete when Jesus returns.

power in prayer are blessings of living a more pure life.[104]

---

[104] These blessings are not earned by purity because access to God comes through Christ. Rather, living in purity removes barriers to greater intimacy and power in prayer because it opens the lines of communication and enables us to experience God's presence in a greater way.

Cultivating Discipline

...O God, thou art my God; early will I seek thee: my soul thirsteth for thee, my flesh longeth for thee in a dry and thirsty land, where no water is; To see thy power and thy glory, so as I have seen thee in the sanctuary. Psalm 63:1-2 KJV

Discipline is essential for your prayer life because forgetting or neglecting to take time for prayer causes you to miss out on your time with God.

Seeking God early in the day is one way to cultivate discipline in your prayer life. Set your alarm clock to go off before the usual time you would wake up so that you can spend time with God. Even if you go to work early, taking ten minutes in the morning will get you started off right. Then, you can schedule an additional time later in the day as needed. Scheduling time with God first thing in the morning means you are less likely to procrastinate or forget to do it. It also helps set the tone for the remainder of the day.

Having a designated place for quiet time is another way to cultivate discipline in your prayer life. Pick a consistent place to have your time with God that is unlikely to have any distractions. People in my family have prayed in the laundry room (Mom said nobody comes in there in the morning!), a closet, a closed room, and even in the local cemetery. I was surprised at the choice of the cemetery, but I have tried it and it works for me.[105] Do what works for you. The Enemy[106] will try to disrupt your time with God if he can, and a good location can help to prevent this.

Be disciplined in this for six weeks, and you will have developed a life-changing habit

---

[105] Only choose places that are secure for you to be. Keeping your eyes open in a public place is wise so that you will notice any risks and avoid them.

[106] Satan and/or his demons will distract. Well-meaning people and family members can also distract. Respond to people with love, but seek a place with minimal distractions because a quiet place will help you focus on God.

Part Four: Improving Your Prayer Life by Starting Well

Starting With Help

Now Jesus was praying in a certain place, and when he finished, one of his disciples said to him, 'Lord, teach us to pray, as John taught his disciples.' Luke 11:1

Ask God for help when you are beginning to pray. This help comes in two ways. You can ask Christ to teach you to pray, and you can ask the Holy Spirit to pray through you.

Jesus is willing to teach you through Scripture and through the example of others. He provides examples of prayer in the Psalms. As you read through the Psalms, you can pray them to God. Praying the Psalms will help you learn to pray powerfully from the heart as well as bring some variety to your prayer life.[107] Other examples of prayer are located throughout the Bible such as Jesus' high priestly prayer in John 17 or Paul's prayers in his epistles (letters) to the churches.[108] Feel free to substitute your own name, the names of others, or the name of your church as the Spirit directs your heart in prayer. Jesus also will teach you to pray when you observe other Spirit-filled believers who pray in your local church assembly.[109] Grow in prayer through their example.

---

[107] For a great book on this, see Donald S. Whitney, *Praying the Bible* (Wheaton: Crossway, 2015).
[108] I.e. Colossians 1:9-12
[109] If you have a group that prays together in your church or if you have the opportunity to meet with a couple of individuals for prayer, take advantage of this. People with a heart for

Ask the Holy Spirit to pray through you or to lead you in your prayers.[110] He will do this by bringing people to mind who need prayer, bringing Scriptures to mind that you can pray to God, or by giving you a burden about something in your life or the lives of others. Pray according to what the Holy Spirit reveals. The Holy Spirit may guide you to pray for a specific need on behalf of another individual, even though you might not have had prior knowledge of that need. Don't share this information with others or even with the individual you have prayed for unless God leads you to do so or you think it would encourage him.

It should encourage you that you have someone who delights to help you in prayer. The Holy Spirit will help you, and Jesus will teach you. Believe this and rest in it. Trust that God can use you in prayer as you follow the Spirit's leading.

---

prayer often are the best people to instruct you and help you grow in prayer.
[110] Ephesians 6:18

Starting With Thanks

...give thanks in all circumstances; for this is the will of God in Christ Jesus for you. 1 Thessalonians 5:18

One of the greatest ways to enrich your prayer life and to begin time with God is to saturate your prayers with thanks to God. When the Jewish people would travel to the Temple in Bible days, they would enter the gates of the city with thanks to God.[111] God taught them of the necessity of thanksgiving through the Psalms and probably also through the leadership of King David as he organized the worship during his reign.[112] They did this to honor God, illustrating how thanking God draws us near to enjoy His presence.

You can thank God for big things and little things. Thank Him for the forgiveness you have through the blood of Jesus. Thank God that He has made it possible for you to enjoy His presence in prayer. Also thank Him for your food, the place you live, the clothes you wear, and the spiritual blessings He gives you. Thank Him for your family, friends, and other believers who encourage you in your relationship with Jesus Christ. Thank Him for answered prayer, His protection, and His guidance in life. Thank Him for the beauty of nature. Ask God to increase your creativity and awareness so that you

---

[111] Psalm 100:4
[112] 1 Chronicles 15:16, 27

can express your gratitude to Him effectively. You can do this in prayer or in music. I like to do both.

If you have been struggling and do not feel like thanking God, thank Him anyway as an act of the will. There is something about thanking God that redirects our hearts toward Him and helps us begin to trust Him.

Starting With Praise

Enter his gates with thanksgiving, and his courts with praise! Give thanks to him; bless his name! Psalm 100:4

Praising God is simply telling Him about His greatness. We enjoy praise as human beings, but God delights in our praise and inhabits the praises of His people.[113] If you want to draw near to God in prayer, spend time praising Him at the beginning of your prayer time. This works better than almost anything else you can do to draw near to God.

To find help in learning to praise God, go to the Psalms in the Bible. They are filled with praise to God and provide guidance through examples. Also, do a study on the names of God, Christ, and the Holy Spirit.[114] You could do a Google search on this. Go to Henry Blackaby's workbook entitled, "Experiencing God."[115] In the back of the workbook, the names of God are listed. Some study bibles may also include them.

We praise when we say something good about God. You could say, "I praise you, God, because you are ____." Whatever comes to mind about God that is good can be made into a statement of praise to Him. The longer you are a Christian, the more you will learn about God and the more you will have

---

[113] Psalm 22:3 KJV
[114] Psalm 76:2
[115] Henry Blackaby and Claude King, *Experiencing God: Knowing and Doing the Will of God* (Nashville: B & H Publishing Group, 1990).

material that you can use to praise Him. Read the Bible. As you read, notice what the Bible says about God and praise Him for the good things He is and the good things He has done.

Here is a brief prayer of praise to God to give you an example of how it might work. Prayer: *God, I praise you for your faithfulness. You are always there for me and always care for me. I praise you that you hear my prayers and that you answer them so many times in my life. I praise you for your great power that is able to change my circumstances and overcome the challenges I face. You made the universe and are in control. Your wisdom is perfect, and your kindness is great. Your mercy and grace give me hope.*

Starting With Spiritual Hunger

Blessed are they which do hunger and thirst after righteousness: for they shall be filled. Matthew 5:6 KJV

You will seek me and find me, when you seek me with all your heart. Jeremiah 29:13

If you come to God with a heart that is hungering for His righteousness[116] and seeking a close relationship with God, this delights Him. If you are just checking a task off your list when you have your quiet time with God, you need to confess this to Him. Ask Him to fill you with the Holy Spirit, and ask the Holy Spirit to love God through you. Ask Him to give you a heart that truly hungers and thirsts for righteousness.

When you fulfill the conditions of the promises in the two verses above, you will reap the promised benefits. The person who hungers and thirsts for righteousness will be filled. And the person who seeks God with all her heart will find Him. Spiritual intimacy with God is improved when we come with the right attitude. Do you want to spend time with people who do not really want to spend time with you? God is no different. He wants us to genuinely desire Him and the righteous life He desires for us.

---

[116] Righteousness is doing the right thing and having a heart that desires the right thing. No one is perfectly righteous but Christ. Yet we can live righteous lives for seasons of time through the power of the Holy Spirit once we have a relationship with God.

Trust the Holy Spirit to love God through you and to hunger for righteousness through you as you ask Him to do so. He delights to help us come into God's presence in the right way.

Starting in a Quiet Place

And after he had dismissed the crowds, he went up on the mountain by himself to pray. When evening came, he was there alone.... Matthew 14:23

You need to find a place where you can be alone with God so that you can seek Him with fewer distractions. If Jesus needed to be alone, we need to be alone. When we are alone, we can pour our hearts out to God and be honest with Him. When we are alone, we can refocus on Him when we have lost our perspective.

Choose to be alone with God so that you can hear Him speak to you through His Spirit and through Scripture. He may convict you of sin, He may give you direction, or He may encourage you with some assurance from His Word.

Decide to be alone with God so that your mind can be renewed.[117] During your time with God, you will be instructed through His Word and changed in your thinking. The alternative is to be conformed to the world's way of thinking.[118]

Elect to be alone with God so that you will be more uninhibited as you speak with Him. Usually, in public or with an audience, we are conscious of what others may think. In our alone time with God, we are caring about what He thinks.

Choose to be alone with God so that you can be refreshed and strengthened for your walk with God.

---

[117] Romans 12:1-2
[118] Matthew 12:34-37; Mark 7:20-23; Luke 6:45

If you let the Holy Spirit guide you in your alone time, you will find that He restores your soul as you spend time with God.[119] He may guide you to a specific Scripture, to listen to a particular worship song, or just to listen quietly for His still small voice to tell you something. Let the Holy Spirit change your routine if He desires so that you spend more time on one thing one day, but perhaps less the next day. He perfectly knows what you need, let Him take the lead. If He is not leading you in any particular way, follow your normal routine.

Decide to be alone with God regularly so that you will not drift in your spiritual life. I have found that if I miss or hurry three days of my time with God, I begin to drift spiritually. I can tell the difference on the first day usually, but I especially can tell the difference after three days. Your time with God is your spiritual lifeline. Do not neglect it.[120]

For these reasons, being alone with God is a great way to begin your time with God well. Being alone prepares you to hear from God. If you are distracted, you are less likely to hear from God or be helped by Him. Ask God to help you focus as you draw aside to be with Him.

---

[119] Psalm 23:3
[120] 1 Peter 5:8

Starting With Expectancy

*And without faith it is impossible to please him,
for whoever would draw near to God must believe
that he exists and that he rewards those who seek
him. Hebrews 11:6*

When we come to meet with God or ask God for
something in our lives, we need to come with an
expectant heart of faith. We cannot please God or
draw near to God without a heart that trusts that He
will reward us for doing so.

I begin my quiet time by asking the Father to fill
me with the Holy Spirit[121] and to surrender and trust
through me. Then I choose to surrender to God, and
I choose to trust in God. The point is that the Spirit
empowers us to trust[122] first, and then we can
choose to trust. Ask the Holy Spirit to have a faith-
filled heart through you, and to come to God
through you with a sense of expectancy.

When you come to God in expectant faith, you
will be rewarded with more answers to prayer, but
especially with greater closeness to God. Begin your
quiet time in expectancy to meet with God, hear
from God, and experience God. Expect the Holy
Spirit to speak to you through the Scripture, and ask
Him to do so. Trust that Christ is eager to help you,
comfort you, and enable you through the time that
you spend with Him.

---

[121] See the chapters below on the Holy Spirit.
[122] See Galatians 5:22-23 for the fruit of the Spirit that includes
faithfulness or, "faith" as it can be translated.

Starting With Honesty

The LORD is near to all who call on him, to all who call on him in truth. He fulfills the desire of those who fear him; he also hears their cry and saves them. Psalm 145:18-19

We need to be honest with God about what we are feeling and thinking when we come to Him in prayer. He knows what we are thinking anyway.

Calling on God in truth means letting Him know when you are struggling. Sometimes I have trouble focusing on God or on the prayers I am praying. I tell God and ask Him to help me focus. Other times I may not want to have my time with God because I am out of sorts or struggling in some way. I tell Him and ask Him to change my heart. Honesty can go a long way in helping you connect with God as you identify your problems and ask God to help you solve them. He delights to do this.

Calling on God in truth requires that we confess any known sin.[123] This helps us by restoring our connection with God relationally. Since our sin grieves God and affects our closeness to God relationally, we need to confess it at the beginning of our prayer time. God has promised to forgive[124] when we confess our sins to Him.

---

[123] 1 John 1:9

[124] The person who knows Christ has already been forgiven the penalties for their sins past, present, and future. The forgiveness mentioned in 1 John is making up with God when something you have done grieves Him. It is a restoring of

Calling on God in truth includes casting your cares on Him.[125] All of us have problems and struggles that we can bring to God. As we persist in praying about the struggles and mix thanksgiving with these prayers, He brings His peace to us.[126]

Calling on God in truth requires that when we tell God something, we really mean it. As you go through your prayer list, you may pray something like, "God, I surrender completely to you." It is easy to say something like this and not truly mean it. If you do this, pray, "I believe, Lord help my unbelief."[127] Ask the Holy Spirit to pray through you so that you can genuinely surrender to God, trust in God, or do whatever God desires.

Finally, we can be honest with God because we are already accepted in Jesus Christ.[128] Since Jesus has already paid for all our sin, we do not have to worry about punishment for something that we tell God. Since God knows already all that we think, we do not have to be worried that He will be disappointed if we tell Him the truth. If[129] you have repented of sin and put your trust in Jesus to give you the gift of eternal life when you asked Him to do

---

fellowship. Our salvation is eternally secure once we have trusted Christ.

[125] 1 Peter 5:7
[126] Philippians 4:6-7
[127] Mark 9:24
[128] Ephesians 1:6-7
[129] This paragraph assumes a person has a relationship with Christ that comes through repentance and faith. See page 37 if you need to begin a relationship with Christ.

so, it is settled. Approach God as a loved child approaches his parents boldly.[130]

Starting With Variety

Is anyone among you suffering? Let him pray. Is anyone cheerful? Let him sing praise. James 5:13

It is common for people to develop a routine for their daily quiet time. Sometimes you may need to alter that routine to address the issues in your heart.

If you are greatly burdened, you may not be able to move on to other things mentally until you tell God about the burden on your heart. Other times, your heart may be full of praise, and you may want to start with singing. Still other times, you may want to hear from God's Word first, asking God to speak to you through it. Occasionally, you may need to confess sin as the first item of business with God. God knows we are at different places emotionally and spiritually at different times. Relax and be yourself with God. Set your normal routine aside. You can return to it later after you respond to God as your heart desires to respond. I have found that ignoring where my heart is sometimes causes me to waste time and results in continued distraction. Listen to the Holy Spirit in this as well. He can help you when you do not know how to start. Changing the order of your quiet time can help to enrich your time with God. Routines are good but can be a hindrance to your relationship with God if you do not practice some flexibility in this.

Are you suffering? Pray. Are you cheerful? Sing praise to God!

Part Five: Improving Your Prayer Life with Supernatural Support

Trusting Your Forerunner

*We have this as a sure and steadfast anchor of
the soul, a hope that enters into the inner place
behind the curtain, where Jesus has gone as a
forerunner on our behalf, having become a high
priest forever after the order of Melchizedek.
Hebrews 6:19-20*

Jesus prepared the way for us to enter God's
presence by first dying on the cross and rising from
the dead. His death on the cross satisfied God's
justice[131] so that He does not have to give us justice
for our sin. Jesus also bore God's wrath on the cross
for our sin and completely satisfied it.[132] Jesus' work
at the cross means we can enter God's presence
boldly because we have nothing to fear. Jesus paid
everything for us to come to God.

Jesus also prepared for us to come into God's
presence by ascending to heaven and by sitting
down at the right hand of God. He prays for us,[133]
and He shows the Father the nail-scars He bore for
us. Since Jesus already has born[134] our sin at the
cross, we are free to come.

God is always happy to see you come to Him in
prayer. Trust in this fact when you pray. Believe that
God receives you because of what Christ has done
for you. Pour out your heart to Him in prayer

---

131 Romans 3:26
132 Romans 3:25; 1 John 2:2
133 Hebrews 7:25
134 Isaiah 53:12 is fulfilled in the work of Jesus.

because He loves us with an everlasting love.[135]
When my kids were little, they would come wanting
to sit on my lap and climb up in the chair without
asking. They knew I was always happy for them to
come. This is the way God wants us to approach
Him. Come with confidence that God loves you. If
you question His love for you, remember the
cross.[136] Hope in the unchanging truth that God's
invitation is always open for you to come to Him in
prayer. Let this truth be the anchor for your soul.[137]

Also, ask Jesus to pray for you and with you. He
is our intercessor.[138]

[135] Jeremiah 31:3
[136] John 3:16
[137] For further explanation on this Scripture, see Roger Pugh, *Hearing God's Voice and Responding in Faith: a Commentary on Hebrews* (Colombia, South Carolina: Createspace, 2017).
[138] Hebrews 7:25

Abiding in Christ

Abide in me, and I in you. As the branch cannot bear fruit by itself, unless it abides in the vine, neither can you, unless you abide in me. I am the vine; you are the branches. Whoever abides in me and I in him, he it is that bears much fruit, for apart from me you can do nothing. John 15:4-5

We can do nothing in our walk with Christ without His supernatural empowerment. This includes our prayer life. We get this empowerment by abiding in Him. As a branch is connected to a vine, we are to be connected to Christ. First, we need to begin a relationship with Him.[139] But once we have a relationship with Him, each day we must choose to abide in Him. Abiding in Christ involves several things.

First, abiding in Christ involves an ongoing sense of dependence on Him and trust in Him. We recognize that we cannot pray or do anything else without Him, and we look to Him in expectancy and trust for Him to supply what we need. You may have a person at your workplace that you rely on to help you get the job done. Christ is the person who helps us pray. Depend on Him and trust Him to do so.

Second, abiding in Christ involves fellowship with Him. This should begin in the morning as we spend time with Him in prayer, worship, and reading the Scripture. It also includes recognition and trust that He is with us throughout the day. A prayer quickly

---

[139] See the chapter, "Receiving a Relationship" on page 37.

offered when a crisis arises, or a prayer of thanks for something good; both are characteristics of abiding in Christ. Listening for the prompting of the Holy Spirit to act or share in some way is part of abiding in Christ as well. We listen and we share as in any human relationship. We live and act as though He were right there with us because He is.[140]

Third, abiding involves surrender to Christ in ongoing obedience.[141] Our obedience to Christ will not be perfect until Jesus returns and we have our sin nature taken away. Yet immediate confession of sin to God and asking God for a right spirit can quickly get us back on the right track. Regular choices of obedience help us walk more fully in Christ.

---

[140] Brother Lawrence called this, "practicing the presence of God." See the book, "The Practice of the Presence of God the Best Rule of a Holy Life: Being Conversations and Letters of Brother Lawrence" http://www.pathsoflove.com/pdf/Practice-of-the-Presence-of-God.pdf (accessed 1/6/18), 3.

[141] John 15:10-12

Pleading the Blood

In him we have redemption through his blood, the forgiveness of our trespasses, according to the riches of his grace.... Ephesians 1:7

But now in Christ Jesus you who once were far off have been brought near by the blood of Christ. Ephesians 2:13

Sometimes I struggle to get started in prayer, and I feel like there is a hindrance to prayer, but I am not sure why. When I have this happen, I have found that simply telling the Lord, "Lord, it seems like there is something wrong in my relationship with you, but I'm not sure what it is. I want to plead the shed blood of Jesus as my means of coming into your presence. His blood covers my sin, even the sin I do not know exists. His blood brings me near. It is not on my own goodness or worthiness that I come to you in prayer. I come based on His perfect goodness and righteousness. I come because His death on the cross paid the price for me to come. I'm not worthy, but I plead the blood!" I have found that many times this works to help me get started. After all, the perfect righteousness of Jesus is pleasing to God and the blood Christ shed covers all our sin.[142] God delights in the finished work of Jesus at the cross so plead the blood! God's grace is so great it can take care of any problem in our relationship through the blood of Jesus.[143] Put all your trust in

---

[142] 1 John 1:7
[143] Hebrews 9:13-14

your forerunner's work to open the way to God's presence.

Relying on the Spirit's Groaning

Likewise the Spirit helps us in our weakness. For we do not know what to pray for as we ought, but the Spirit himself intercedes for us with groanings too deep for words. And he who searches hearts knows what is the mind of the Spirit, because the Spirit intercedes for the saints according to the will of God. Romans 8:26-27

If you feel inadequate to pray, know that the Holy Spirit helps you with prayer. There have been times where I thought I did not know how to pray about a specific issue or did not think that words were enough to express what was in my heart. The Holy Spirit helps us with this. He takes what we cannot express to God and expresses it to Him with groanings that cannot be spoken. If your pain is too great for you to articulate, ask the Holy Spirit to pray for you. If your confusion is too great, ask the Holy Spirit to express clearly what is needed to God.

When you feel that you do not know what God's will is concerning something in your life, the Holy Spirit can help you with that as well. He will pray for you according to the perfect will of God. You can also ask Him to lead you[144] and give you wisdom[145] in the circumstances you are facing.

Also, know that God is the searcher of your heart. He can take bad grammar and poorly expressed words and translate them according to what He sees

---

[144] John 16:13
[145] Isaiah 11:2; Ephesians 1:17

in your heart. You do not have to use big words or King James English to communicate with God. Just come sincerely, trusting that He knows your heart. Communicate with God the way you normally communicate with other people. As the searcher of hearts, He also knows the heart of the Holy Spirit so that the Spirit's groanings are perfectly clear to Him. Everything that the Holy Spirit asks for you will be given because God understands and always responds to Him. The Holy Spirit will only pray for you according to what God desires for your good and for God's purpose for your life.[146]

---

[146] Romans 8:28. Of course, this praying of the Holy Spirit is for those who have received this relationship with God through Jesus. See page 37.

Part Six: Improving Your Prayer Life by Praying with Other People

Praying with Prayer Partners

Again I say to you, if two of you agree on earth about anything they ask, it will be done for them by my Father in heaven. For where two or three are gathered in my name, there am I among them.
Matthew 18:19-20

God encourages us to have prayer partners by telling us of the power of praying with them. Anything we ask God to give while praying together, He delights to answer. It is assumed that the individuals desire to please God and desire His will. If this condition is met, there is supernatural potential to our times of prayer. I have seen God accomplish things that I knew were humanly impossible such as solving church problems, seeing sick people healed, and seeing unreceptive people won to faith in Christ. All things are possible with God, and God's power is released when we pray.

Praying with a prayer partner helps you grow in prayer. Since every believer has different spiritual gifts,[147] their gifts are often expressed in their prayers. I have a friend who has the spiritual gift of faith. As I prayed with him over the years, my faith was strengthened. Perhaps you are praying with someone who has the gift of teaching. Chances are that you will learn some new things about God's Word as he or she prays God's Word. Maybe you are praying with someone who has the gift of

---

[147] See 1 Corinthians 12, Ephesians 4:11-16, and Romans 12:4-8.

discernment. You may grow in your discernment as you consider the things being prayed. Praying with prayer partners helps us to grow because we learn from each other.

Also, praying with a prayer partner helps fill in the gaps of our prayers. Sometimes we may not pray about specific issues or even consider those issues until we hear someone else praying about them. Differences in our gifts, progress in spiritual growth, and personalities will result in different emphases in our prayers. As someone with different giftedness prays for you, he or she may bring up things you never would think to mention about your life.[148]

Prayer partners are also an encouragement.[149] Many times when struggling, I have prayed with a prayer partner and have been greatly refreshed. This does not always happen. But I have found that certain people who pray led by the Holy Spirit will bring refreshment to your soul.[150]

Ask God to lay a person or a couple of individuals on your heart to ask to be prayer partners. Meet weekly or at least monthly so that you can join together in prayer. Do not ask a gossip or a critical person to be a prayer partner. Find a person that loves Christ and loves people. Let your sharing of concerns be confidential, and only share what is necessary to pray. Do not let prayer request time be a gossip session. You may mention a person without even discussing the specific problem or you may

---

[148] Ezra motivated the Israelites to pray prayers of repentance through his burdened prayer. See Ezra 10:1.
[149] Philemon 1:4-7; Luke 11:1
[150] Ecclesiastes 4:10

share generally, as the Lord leads you to share. Sometimes, I have not even mentioned the need except to say that the Lord knows what I'm asking to receive. You may have times where you have no specific requests, but you can worship and thank God for what He has done. Praising and thanking God in prayer is the best part of praying with a prayer partner.

Praying Corporately

All these with one accord were devoting themselves to prayer, together with the women and Mary the mother of Jesus, and his brothers. Acts 1:14

Corporate prayer is a powerful tool to help with spiritual growth and with the struggles of the Christian life. It also helps with entering into fellowship with other believers on a deeper level.

Of course, there have been times when all of us have been in a boring prayer meeting. I have noticed that prayer becomes boring when it is ritual focused rather than relationship focused. If people pray the same prayers verbatim every time or merely list requests, a focus on God is lacking, and the prayer becomes dry. If you are in a church that prays this way, you can set an example, and God may change your church's prayer culture over time. Either way, if you are praying in the right way, you will bless others through your prayers, and you will be blessed. I hesitate to use the words, "praying the right way" because God wants us to come to Him where we are, and He delights in us coming to Him if we come with sincerity and a surrendered heart. Yet corporate prayer is different because it involves other people. If corporate prayer is done ritually and with a focus merely on requests, it will seem dry. But if it is focused on God and led by the Spirit, it will become vital, encouraging, and edifying for God's people. There are several things you can do to infuse life and edification into your prayer times.

First, focus on God through prayers of praise[151] and thanksgiving.[152] Thanking and praising God helps us in several ways. It helps us with having our primary focus on God, but it also helps us by reminding us of how good God is and who He is. Often we come to a prayer meeting burdened by the struggles of the day. Focusing on God's character and divine attributes helps us have perspective and promotes faith rather than fear. Ask God for what you need, but mix it with a generous dose of praise and thanksgiving.[153]

Second, let it be Spirit-led.[154] Ask the Holy Spirit to pray through you and guide you in your prayers. Let Him lead you to pray specific prayers for specific needs in the church, in the lives of God's people, and in the community. Since the Holy Spirit is the Comforter, following His lead in prayer means that He will use you to comfort others who are gathered in the prayer meeting. Often God will speak into someone's life about something that they have not even shared with the group. People begin to realize that God is meeting with them and they are profoundly encouraged as God ministers to them through the prayers of their brothers and sisters in Christ. If you struggle with discerning the Spirit's

---

[151] Praise is telling God how great He is, usually by mentioning some specific attribute such as His perfect wisdom or His mercy that is new every morning.

[152] Thanks is just saying thank you to God for specific things He has done.

[153] See the earlier chapters on worshipping with praise and worshipping with thanksgiving.

[154] "Praying in every opportunity in the Spirit" - Ephesians 6:18

leading, ask Him to do this in your private prayer time as practice.[155] If God lays someone on your heart during your time with Him, let him or her know (if it is wise and edifying to do so). Include specifics of what God led you to pray. As I have done this, I have gotten great feedback from people that what I prayed for them was exactly their struggle. Other times, they just say thank you. But you can get some positive feedback that will help you while encouraging your brothers and sisters in Christ by letting them know that you are praying and that God has laid them on your heart. One powerful thing about this is that God can use you to pray for things that a person might never share with you. In those cases, keep it to yourself.

Third, if you are leading the meeting, let people know that they can pray a sentence prayer to God.[156] Prayers do not have to be long to be edifying or effective. Also, let people know that they do not have to use King James English in prayer. Tell them they can be themselves and that God just wants them to come to Him sincerely and to speak from the heart.

Fourth, pray your burdens from the heart. Do not feel as though you have to cover every request that has been offered in corporate prayer.[157] Let the Spirit put His burden on your heart and pray it. Most people cannot remember everything that has been mentioned anyway.

---

[155] This is an excellent practice anyway and sorely needed.
[156] See the book by Daniel Henderson, *Prayzing* (Colorado Springs: NavPress, 2007), 66.
[157] Usually the leader is writing things down and will do this.

Fifth, stop when the Spirit leads you to stop. Praying long prayers for show quenches the Spirit, and you lose your reward.[158] Do not feel pressure to keep your prayer within time constraints as this can also quench the Spirit.

Sixth, if you are leading the prayer time, let people share what God is doing. This can bring encouragement through reports of answered prayer, but can also reveal needs that need to be lifted to the Lord.

Seventh, look at corporate prayer as a time to meet with God more than as a time to get what you want. Scripture says if we delight ourselves in the Lord, He will give us the desires of our hearts.[159] Meeting with God is what makes a prayer meeting come alive. I recently had someone come to me and tell me how much the prayers at our prayer meeting encouraged him in his struggle. He said, "God ministered to me. I could feel it!" This is what God-focused corporate prayer will do.

---

[158] Matthew 6:5-8
[159] Psalm 37:4

Praying with Your Family

...do not be anxious about anything, but in everything by prayer and supplication with thanksgiving let your requests be made known to God. And the peace of God, which surpasses all understanding, will guard your hearts and your minds in Christ Jesus. Philippians 4:6-7 [160]

Family prayer is important for several reasons. We support and strengthen our families, we protect our families, we teach our children, we encourage each other, and we find God's peace as a family through prayer.

Anxiety and trouble come to every family. In those times, we have an opportunity to come together for prayer to provide support and strength for each other. We sense that we are facing the trouble together when we pray. Many times, I have come to my family with a request, or they have come to me. It is amazing how God binds us together and strengthens us when we pray. As we grow closer to God, we grow closer to each other. [161]

---

[160] These verses are often considered to apply only to individuals. I have often used it myself in this way, but the pronouns are actually plural in the original language indicating that praying together is one way this Scripture can be used. I have seen the truths of this passage lived out in my family.
[161] The illustration of a triangle is often used to show that we grow closer together as we grow closer to God. I'm not sure where this illustration initially came from, but I have heard it from many sources.

God's peace guards our hearts and minds when we pray together. Whether Satan has come against us, or people are against us, we are guarded by God and kept in His peace as we take our burdens to Him with thanksgiving as a family.

Our children learn how to pray as they see us model prayer. As dad and mom pour out their hearts to God with thanksgiving, God brings peace and prayers are answered. Answers are celebrated, and children learn that prayer truly changes things. They learn how to walk in faith rather than fear, and they are taught the path to God's peace.

We encourage each other when we pray together as a family. Prayer itself is an encouragement because we understand that someone is asking God to help us. But if we are praying under the direction of the Holy Spirit, God can use the words of our prayers to encourage those who are listening. Many times, I have been profoundly encouraged as I listened to the Spirit-filled prayers of a family member. Ask God to fill you with the Spirit and pray through you so that your prayers will encourage your family members. Pay attention to Scriptures God brings to mind or to specific requests you sense a need to address. While our prayers are directed to God and are primarily for Him, God uses our prayers to build up our families. Praying Scripture as God brings it to mind or thanking God for His name[162] as it applies to our situation are ways that

---

[162] If you are praying about a sickness, you could thank God that He is Jehovah/Yahweh Rapha, the great I AM who heals us. If you are fearful, you could thank God that He has

God might encourage both you and your family members when you pray.

Prayer with thanksgiving brings God's peace to families. When my family has been especially burdened about something, we have prayed and found peace despite the difficult situation. God has a way of lifting burdens through thankful prayer. Choosing to thank Him in trouble redirects our thinking to God's faithfulness. Telling God what is wrong reminds us that God is for us,[163] loves us,[164] and is able to help us in times of trouble.[165] Take your burdens to Him as a family and thank Him, you will discover that He can bring peace to your soul as you look to Him in faith and pray.

For those whose families are unsaved or unwilling to pray together, know that you are part of the family of God. Find some good prayer partners in your church or elsewhere who are willing to pray for you when things are hard. Also, pray for the salvation and transformation of your family members. With God, all things are possible.[166]

---

promised never to leave us or forsake us and you could praise Him for His faithfulness.

[163] Romans 8:28, 31
[164] Romans 8:35-37
[165] Psalm 46:1
[166] Mark 10:27

88

Praying With the Church Leaders

Is anyone among you sick? Let him call for the elders of the church, and let them pray over him, anointing him with oil in the name of the Lord. And the prayer of faith will save the one who is sick, and the Lord will raise him up. And if he has committed sins, he will be forgiven. James 5:14-15

When a serious illness comes, we can ask the leadership of the church to pray for us. Elders are pastors. But in a single pastor church, pastors and deacons could be asked to pray. The anointing with oil is a symbol of the fact that the Holy Spirit's touch brings healing. Then, as the elders pray in faith, the Lord will raise him up from his sick bed and forgive any sin that may have been the reason for sickness.[167]

I have seen this work in the local church setting, but this is not twisting God's arm. If God has some purpose for allowing the sickness, He can overrule the prayer and allow it to continue.[168]

In my daughter's case, the healing came through medication that enabled her to live with the illness, and only after several years was complete healing accomplished. Then medicine was no longer necessary.

---

[167] This probably refers to chastening or discipline from God for an ongoing sin. See Hebrews 12:5-11. However, it could even apply to a sin unknown to the individual. Compare Mark 2:5-12.

[168] 2 Corinthians 12:7-9

Calling for the leaders of the church seems to imply that special effectiveness comes in this type of prayer, but God is still able to answer with yes, no, or wait.

Confessing Your Faults to One Another

Therefore, confess your sins to one another and pray for one another, that you may be healed. The prayer of a righteous person has great power as it is working. Elijah was a man with a nature like ours, and he prayed fervently that it might not rain, and for three years and six months it did not rain on the earth. Then he prayed again, and heaven gave rain, and the earth bore its fruit. My brothers, if anyone among you wanders from the truth and someone brings him back, let him know that whoever brings back a sinner from his wandering will save his soul from death and will cover a multitude of sins. James 5:16-20

Praying together can be preceded by sharing faults or struggles. When we feel overwhelmed by our sin, we can bear each other's burdens.[169] Sharing should be general rather than specific. Share enough information so that prayer can be offered, but reliving the sin in detail does not help. The prayer is for healing for a specific sin and for overcoming the sin's bondage or hold over that person's life. This prayer also assumes the person already has a relationship with Jesus Christ.[170]

Confession should be made to someone that we trust and who does not have a tendency to gossip. Ask God to help you choose a spiritually mature

---

[169] Galatians 6:2
[170] See page 37 if you need to begin a relationship with Jesus Christ.

person who is both loving and willing to help with this kind of prayer. Confidentiality is essential so that God has time to work in our hearts.[171]

Prayer should be made with fervency and trust. God stopped the rain for three years and then restarted it through the fervent prayer of Elijah. As we pray with fervency and trust, God can bring a sinner back from the error of his ways and cover a multitude of sins.

---

[171] Some matters such as child abuse or suicide must be or may be reported by law. Also, if someone else would be hurt or the church would be hurt by withholding the information, safety should be the priority over silence. Letting the person know that whatever does not harm others, the church, or the individual will be held confidential can be helpful in understanding your commitment and its limits. Those in official offices such as counselors or clergy may want to get information from experts or seek legal counsel as to how to proceed and communicate.

Part Seven: Improving Your Prayer Life When You are Struggling

Struggling With Speaking

...I am so troubled that I cannot speak. Psalm 77:4

Remember that God loves you when you are too troubled to speak. He is a kind heavenly father who understands our frailties.[172] God does not point a finger at us or berate us when we struggle. Instead, He helps us.[173]

Sometimes we have trouble speaking because we do not know what to say. When you feel this way, ask God to fill you with the Holy Spirit and pray through you.[174] Then pray what He leads you to pray. Ask the Lord Jesus and the Holy Spirit to pray to the Father according to His perfect will. Another option is opening to the Psalms and choosing one that fits your situation. Then pray that psalm to God.

Sometimes we have trouble speaking because we are emotionally overwhelmed. When you feel this way, ask God to supply what you need even if you don't know what you need. You could pray something like this, "Lord, I'm not sure what I need, but I am really struggling. Would you please supply what I need spiritually and emotionally to help me pray, live for you, and relate to you?"

Sometimes we have trouble speaking because we are under spiritual attack from Satan or his demons.

---

[172] Psalm 103:14
[173] Psalm 121:1-2
[174] Ephesians 6:18; Jude 1:20

The Enemy can implant a thought in our mind[175] or an accusation that leads us to believe a lie.[176] Ask God to give you discernment to recognize this when this happens in your life. Ask God to reveal His truth to you about your situation. The truth will set you free.[177]

---

[175] 2 Corinthians 10:3-5
[176] John 8:44
[177] John 8:32

Struggling With Delayed Answers

I consider the days of old, the years long ago. I said, "Let me remember my song in the night; let me meditate in my heart." Then my spirit made a diligent search: "Will the Lord spurn forever, and never again be favorable? Has his steadfast love forever ceased? Are his promises at an end for all time? Has God forgotten to be gracious? Has he in anger shut up his compassion?" Selah. Then I said, "I will appeal to this, to the years of the right hand of the Most High." I will remember the deeds of the LORD; yes, I will remember your wonders of old. I will ponder all your work, and meditate on your mighty deeds. Psalm 77:5-12

One great struggle is when God delays to answer your prayers or says no to a request. If the issue is important to you, it can bring doubts and cause you to question God's love for you. But God's no's and delays are intended for our good.[178] Sometimes God has a strategic purpose for our suffering or difficulty such as with Paul's thorn in the flesh. He asked God to remove it three times, but God said no because His grace would be sufficient to carry Paul and because His power is perfected in weakness.[179]

When you are struggling with delayed answers, remember other answered prayers, blessings, and

---

[178] Romans 8:28
[179] 2 Corinthians 12:7-9

joys God has given you. If you have been saved[180] for several years, remember the good times and the great things that God has done in the past. This will help restore your perspective. Thank God for the good things He has done, and your attitude will change.

When you are struggling with delayed answers, remember that God's ways are greater than ours and His thoughts as well.[181] Ponder what He has done, and meditate on His mighty actions in the past. God delivered Israel from Egypt and brought them into the Promised Land. The path was not always easy, but God had a plan that He was working to achieve. His ultimate purpose was a blessing for them. Jesus raised the dead and calmed the sea with a mere word. He can handle what you are facing.

Ask the Holy Spirit to help you have a heart that is surrendered to God and trusting in God despite the delays you face in your life. Remember that God uses delays in our lives often as preparation for what He has for us in the future.

Never forget that God has eternal purposes for us. If you are struggling with life the way it is, know that Christ is preparing a place for us[182] where there is no sorrow, crying, pain, sickness, or death.[183] The curse

---

[180] See page 37 if you have questions as to what, "saved" means.
[181] Isaiah 55:8-9
[182] John 14:3
[183] Revelation 21:1-5

of sin will be forever gone,[184] and we will reign with Christ.[185]

---

[184] Romans 8:18-25
[185] Revelation 20:6; 2 Timothy 2:12

Struggling With Perspective

Your way, O God, is holy. What god is great like our God? You are the God who works wonders; you have made known your might among the peoples. You with your arm redeemed your people, the children of Jacob and Joseph. Selah. When the waters saw you, O God, when the waters saw you, they were afraid; indeed, the deep trembled. The clouds poured out water; the skies gave forth thunder; your arrows flashed on every side. The crash of your thunder was in the whirlwind; your lightnings lighted up the world; the earth trembled and shook. Your way was through the sea, your path through the great waters; yet your footprints were unseen. You led your people like a flock by the hand of Moses and Aaron. Psalm 77:13-20

Blessed be the God and Father of our Lord Jesus Christ! According to his great mercy, he has caused us to be born again to a living hope through the resurrection of Jesus Christ from the dead, to an inheritance that is imperishable, undefiled, and unfading, kept in heaven for you, who by God's power are being guarded through faith for a salvation ready to be revealed in the last time. 1 Peter 1:3-5

Sometimes when we are struggling, we just need to remember to consider who God is and what He has prepared for us as His children.

First, we need to remember who He is. He is the God who works wonders and split the Red Sea. The storms, clouds, and lightning bolts obey His commands. His leadership is perfect, and His counsel is sure. He is the all-powerful, all-knowing God who loves us and cares for us as a shepherd cares for His sheep.[186] Read Isaiah 40 to see how God comforts us and cares for us as His people. Consider the creation in Genesis 1-2, and think about all of His power in creating all that is. Read John 3:16 and remember that He sent His Son for you. He truly cares for you. Once you have considered these things, turn these thoughts into worship. Regardless of your circumstances, God remains the same. Praise Him for His majesty, and thank Him for His faithfulness even if it does not seem evident to you right now.

Second, we need to remember that God has saved us in mercy and has prepared an eternal inheritance for us. This inheritance is being stored up right now for us. One day, in an instant, everything will change, and we will be ushered into God's presence and receive the inheritance that we long to receive. Thank Him for what He is doing in heaven on your behalf, and praise Him for your hope. Look up, and be encouraged. God is not finished with you yet.

Third, keep praying. The difficult and dark times are the times we need Him the most. Remember Jesus' heart toward Mary and Martha when their

---

[186] Psalm 23; John 10:11

brother Lazarus had died.[187] He is moved by your struggle, and He understands.[188]

---

[187] John 11:35 - We know this shows Jesus' heart for Mary and Martha because He was going to raise Lazarus from the dead.
[188] Hebrews 4:15

Also by Roger Pugh

Hearing God's Voice and Responding in Faith, A Commentary on Hebrews

Available now on Kindle and in Paperback

34397191R00061

Made in the USA
Lexington, KY
22 March 2019